OLYSLAGER AUTO LIBRARY

American Cars of the 1940s

compiled by the OLYSLAGER ORGANISATION

edited by Bart H. Vanderveen

FREDERICK WARNE & Co Ltd
London and New York

Library of Congress Catalog Card Number 75-186747

ISBN 0 7232 1465 4

Photoset and printed in Great Britain by BAS Printers Ltd, Wallop, Hampshire

American cars of the nineteen-forties are still fairly fresh in the minds of car enthusiasts of today and many are still in existence all over the world.

Like 'American Cars of the 1930s', its predecessor, this volume is intended to serve as a model guide to identify the cars of this period by 'model year', with the accent, again, on the more popular makes.

During the 1930s the cars produced in North America (the United States and Canada) progressed through many basic changes, especially in regard to body styling. The following decade also saw big changes, but in a very different pattern. During 1939–1941 annual changes and restyling of bodywork took place in much the same way as before, but in the middle of the 1942 'model year' production of passenger cars came to an abrupt, albeit not unpredicted, halt as a consequence of America's direct involvement in the Second World War. From then until 1945 the American automobile industry contributed a vast amount of equipment to the war effort, varying from bullets to bombers, in addition, of course, to very large numbers of tanks, trucks, tractors and other motor vehicles.

During this unhappy period the automotive industry of the United States furnished war materials to a value of 29 billion dollars, which amounted to about 20% of the total national output, and more than any other single industry.

As one result of the war effort, the diversification of production and the chronic need for new cars at the end of it, the models brought out as '1946 models' were in fact face-lifted 1942 editions and it was not until 1948 that the 'big three' announced their first true post-war designs. These were almost completely new and went into production as 1949 models, to be continued with only comparatively minor changes for 1950 and 1951. The 'independents', however, had introduced their new models earlier, spearheaded by the very advanced and trend-setting cars of Studebaker (styled by Raymond Loewy) and Kaiser-Frazer (styled by Howard Darrin). Although these were termed 1947 models, they went into production during 1946.

Undoubtedly the most famous of vehicles to emerge from World War II was the 'Jeep'. Cashing in on its world-wide popularity as a reliable and rugged little workhorse, Willys-Overland, its principal producer, wasted no time in introducing a civilian ('de-militarized') version for multi-purpose use at home and overseas, and it did not take long for manufacturers in other countries to either apply for production licences or to copy the basic design. Willys-Overland also launched other Jeep-inspired models, including station wagons.

Post-1945 American cars had lost nothing of their international image of sturdiness, reliability and comfort, and unlike today the products of General Motors, Ford, Chrysler and the smaller automakers still had their own distinctive characteristics and their individual approach to certain technical design concepts.

Piet Olyslager, MSIA, MSAE, KIVI

1940

The Second World War caused the end of civilian car and truck production in US manufacturers' European plants but domestic production was well up on 1939 and sales totalled 3,717,385 cars and 754,901 trucks and buses (compared with 2,888,512 and 700,377 respectively in 1939). Most 1940 models had restyled bodywork. Among the innovations were sealed-beam headlights, and concealed running boards were generally adopted. Military production was also stepped up. In addition to fulfilling European orders for military trucks, production for national defence was increased. To direct this production, William S. Knudsen, president of General Motors, moved to Washington at the invitation of President Roosevelt. Dodge received contracts for 20,000 trucks for the US Army and the first 'Jeep' was produced by American Bantam. The Automotive Committee for Air Defense was formed on 30 October to facilitate aircraft production, and Ford and Packard were contracted for the manufacture of Pratt & Whitney and Rolls-Royce Merlin aircraft engines respectively.

4B Buick

On eating your cake
...AND HAVING IT TOO

It may be true that to those who buy cars in the Buick LIMITED's price range, cost is a matter of importance secondary to comfort, spaciousness, and richness of finish.

But it is certainly worth any man's noting that purchasers of this finest of all the Buicks

consistently report that they can pay for the car *and* a pleasant vacation trip besides for what the equal of this giant-powered, coil-spring-cushioned eighteen-footer would cost them in other places.

Your dealer has a richly illustrated brochure

describing the Buick LIMITED which he will gladly leave with you for study pending the time when you can conveniently try the LIMITED yourself.

"Best buy's Buick!"
EXEMPLAR OF GENERAL MOTORS VALUE

4C Buick

4A
American
Bantam

4A: **American Bantam**, producer of Austin Seven-inspired baby cars, was the first to come up with a military '$\frac{1}{4}$-ton 4 × 4' field car, in the summer of 1940. This new type of vehicle became known as 'Jeep'.
4B: **Buick** in 1940 produced well over 300,000 cars in six series: 40 Special, 50 Super, 60 Century, 70 Roadmaster, 80 and 90 Limited, varying in price from $895 to $2465. Shown is the Series 40 Special Convertible Phaeton (Model 41-C).
4C: Period advertisement of **Buick** Limited limousines. Series 80 had 133-in, Series 90 140-in wheelbase.

5A: The **Cadillac** 1940 line consisted of two LaSalles (q.v.) and five Cadillacs. Included was the Sixty Special which had first been introduced for the 1939 model year. Only the most expensive ($5140) Cadillac had a V16 engine; all the others had V8s. Shown is the Imperial Sedan.

5B: This stylish taxicab was a product of the **Checker** Cab Co., a specialist taxicab builder since the early 1920s.

5C: General Motors' 25-millionth car, a **Chevrolet** sedan, came off the line in 1940. Shown at the ceremony are, from left to right: M. E. Coyle, General Manager of Chevrolet, William S. Knudsen, GM President, Alfred P. Sloan Jr, Chairman of the Board of GM, and Charles E. Wilson, Executive Vice-President of GM. Chevrolet as a Division, incidentally, in 1940 produced its 16-millionth car within ten months after No. 15,000,000! It was the world's largest producer of cars and trucks.

5B Checker Cab

5A Cadillac

5C Chevrolet

6A/B: **Chevrolet** Special DeLuxe Convertible, Series KA. Engine was 216 CID 'Stove Bolt Six', wheelbase 113 in. Convertible top was power-operated and actuated by a control on the dashboard.
6C: Australian **Chevrolet** consisted of Canadian chassis with Holden bodywork which differed in styling from the parent design. There were two versions: Pullman 1200 and Ridemaster 1000.
6D: Australian-built **Chevrolet** Station Wagon used by Australian Army in Egypt. Official nomenclature: 'Car, 6-Passenger, Utility (Aus)'. Note military features: opening windshield and oversize tyres.

6A Chevrolet

6C Chevrolet (Australia)

6B Chevrolet

6D Chevrolet (Australia)

7A: **Chrysler** Saratoga Model C-26S was performance version of New Yorker (C-26N). 323·5 CID 8-in-line engine. Wheelbase 128½ in.
7B: **Chrysler** Crown Imperial Model C-27 was top-line model on 145½-in wb and had Fluid Drive, overdrive, and PAB as standard equipment.

7C: Fluid Drive hydraulic clutch was available on all **Chrysler** Corp. cars except Plymouth and Plymouth-based DeSotos and Dodges. Chrysler also introduced safety-rim wheels and two-leading-shoe front brakes.

7A Chrysler

7B Chrysler Imperial

7C Chrysler

8A DeSoto

8B DeSoto

8C Dodge

8A: **DeSoto** came in two series : the S-7 DeLuxe (shown) and Custom with 122½-in wb, and a special export version SP-9 with 117½-in wb. The latter was mechanically similar to the Plymouth. CID 201·3 and 217·8 respectively.

8B: **DeSoto** Custom S-7 Convertible Coupé displayed in American DeSoto/Plymouth dealer's showroom.

8C: **Dodge** had three model ranges : D-14 Luxury Liner DeLuxe (119½- and 139-in wb), D-15 (117½-in wb export model, based on Plymouth) and D-17 Luxury Liner Special (119½-in wb). The Plymouth-based models had 3⅛ × 4⅜-in bore and stroke, as against 3¼ × 4⅜ for the regular versions. Shown : D-14 Convertible.

9A Ford

9B Ford/M.-H.

9C Ford

9D Ford (Australia)

9A: **Ford** produced its 28-millionth vehicle on 8 April 1940. There were three car chassis: the basic 022A 60 HP, the 01A Standard 85 HP and the 01A DeLuxe 85 HP (all V8s), and 12 body styles.
9B **Ford** Model 01A-73B DeLuxe Fordor with Marmon-Herrington all-wheel drive conversion serving as military staff car in South America.
9C : **Ford** 01A-73B with oversize (9·00—13) tyres in British Army Service.
9D : **Ford** Model 01A-73A Standard Fordor Sedan and 01C Commercial (both 112-in wb, 85 HP) of Australian Army.

10A: **Hudson** Six Coupé had 92-bhp engine, 113-in wb. A sedan set new AAA records for endurance by travelling 20,327 miles at an average of 70·5 mph at Bonneville, Utah.

10B: **Hudson** Eight Convertible Coupé. In 1940 Hudson introduced coil-spring IFS and Weathermaster fresh air and heat control.

10C: Australian Army **Hudson** Eight with ambulance bodywork.

10D: **Hupmobile** Skylark sedan shared bodywork with Graham's Hollywood. The body dies were acquired from Cord after that company ceased operating, but unlike the Cord these cars had conventional rear wheel drive.

10A Hudson

10C Hudson

10B Hudson

10D Hupmobile

11A: **LaSalle**, Cadillac's lower-price line, was discontinued in 1940. In its last year there were two series: the 40-50 and 40-60, the four-passenger coupés of which sold at $1240 and $1380 respectively. Both had V8 engines.

11B: **Lincoln**, Ford's luxury marque, came in two basic models, the 06H Zephyr and the top-line Continental. The Continental Cabriolet cost $2840. Engines were V12. Shown is the Lincoln-Zephyr Coupé.

11C: **Mercury**, Ford's medium price range, was in its second model year. The 100,000th Mercury was produced on 18 January. Designated 09A all 1940 models had 116-in wb and there were five body styles. Shown: 09A-74 Convertible Sedan.

11D: **Mercury** Model 09A-76 Club Convertible, preserved in the USA.

11A LaSalle

11C Mercury

11B Lincoln-Zephyr

11D Mercury

12A: **Nash** Ambassador Eight, Model 4081 Convertible, had 125-in wb. Cheapest Nash products were LaFayettes (from $795), with 117-in wb. After 1940 these were replaced by the '600' line.

12B: **Oldsmobile** Series 60 Club Coupé. Olds offered three series: 60, 70 and 90. Total production in 1940 was 215,028 units and the Hydramatic four-speed automatic transmission was offered as optional equipment for all models.

12C: **Packard** 110 was lowest-price Packard. A DeLuxe version was added for 1940. It sold for $1116 as compared with $1056 for the 110 Special (both 100-bhp 6-cyl. four-door sedans). Packard also introduced an Electromatic Clutch.

12D: **Packard** 120 differed from 110 mainly in having an 8-cyl. engine (4·62-litre, 120 bhp). Wheelbase was 127 in (122 in for 110). Touring sedan shown cost $1261. Also 160 and 180 Super Eight models.

12A Nash

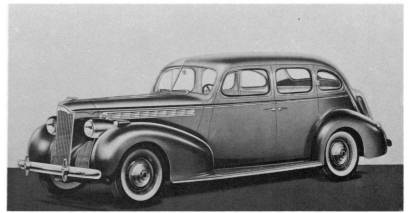

12C Packard

12B Oldsmobile

12D Packard

13A: Plymouth offered two basic ranges: P-9 Road King and P-10 DeLuxe. Both had 117½-in wb and 201·3 CID 84-bhp six-cyl. engine. An 87-bhp engine was optional, as was an economy power unit with low (5·2:1) compression ratio, developing 65 bhp. P-9 was also available as DeSoto and Dodge, with different front end styling.

13B: Plymouth P-10 DeLuxe 'five-window' Club Coupé. At the other end of the range was a seven-passenger sedan.

13C: Surviving 1940 **Plymouth** Sedan in Czechoslovakia, 1968. Car has been modified in some minor details.

13B Plymouth

13A Plymouth

13C Plymouth

1940

14A: Pontiac DeLuxe Two-Door Touring Sedan, Series 26 (6-cyl.) and 28 (8-cyl.). Like Oldsmobile, Pontiac used same basic frame for 6- or 8-cyl. engine. Supporting radiator frame or longer fan shroud made up the difference in shorter engine. In addition to the 120-in wb 26 and 28, there were 117-in wb Special Six, Series 25, and 122-in wb Torpedo Eight, Series 29, models.

14B: Studebaker Champion had 110-in wb and differed from 1939 models in minor details (restyled grille and trim features). RHD Coupé shown.

14C: Studebaker Commander and President were similar in appearance except for nameplates and wheel hub covers. Commander had 6-cyl. 226 CID engine and 116½-in wb, President had 8-in-line 250 CID engine, 122-in wb. Front suspension was independent with transversal leaf spring. Shown: President Coupé.

14D: Willys offered this compact 102-in wb Model 440 sedan with alligator-type hood (bonnet) and front-hinged doors. Several other body styles were available.

14A Pontiac

14C Studebaker

14B Studebaker

14D Willys

This was the last full-production 'model year' before the US became directly involved in World War II as a result of Japan's attack on Pearl Harbor on 7 December. Although military vehicle production was on the increase, more civilian vehicles were sold than in 1940, namely 3,779,682 cars and 1,060,820 trucks and buses. Canadian plants were engaged on production of military vehicles for the British Commonwealth. In the US at least three car makers broke production records. Ford produced its 29-millionth unit, Dodge its 5-millionth, Plymouth its 4-millionth. The number of commercial trucks and buses sold was the highest ever.

More prototypes for the 'Jeep' had been produced by Bantam, Ford and Willys, and they each received contracts for 1500 units for further evaluation and field trials. Chrysler, General Motors and others received further contracts for military trucks from the US Government and several other nations.

15C Buick

15D Buick

15A
American Bantam

15B Buick

15A: **American Bantam** went all out on production of their ¼-ton 4 × 4 and endeavoured to join forces with Checker Cab, but in the end Willys and Ford with their much higher production capacity were awarded the contracts for mass production of the Willys design. The dust-covered Model 40BRC shown was found in the Bantam factory when the company's grounds and buildings were bought by Armco Steel Co. in 1956 (the remaining assets were purchased by Pressed Metals of America, Inc.).

15B: **Buick** Series 50 Super Convertible Phaeton. In 1941 Buick introduced the Fireball engines with increased horsepower.

15C: **Buick** Station Wagon, utilized as Field Grade Officers Staff Car (North Africa).

15D: **Buick** top line model was the Series 90 Limited. Altogether in 1941 Buick offered 26 models in five series.

1941

16A: **Cadillac** announced production of 150-bhp V8s only. V16 and LaSalle were discontinued. All body interiors were now styled by Fleetwood. Hydramatic drive was optional on all models. Model ranges : 61, 62, 63, 60S, 67 and 75. Shown : Series 62 Convertible.

16B: **Cadillac** Series 61 Touring Sedan with 'fast-back' body styling. DeLuxe version had rear wheel shields.

16C: **Chevrolet** Series AG Master DeLuxe had 116-in wb and new body styling which was retained until 1948 (with slight detail changes).

16D: **Chevrolet** Series AH Special DeLuxe had more luxurious trim than Series AG. This RHD Convertible served with the British RAF in Singapore in 1948. Australian Chevies were designated Special DeLuxe 1000 (4110S), Ridemaster 1200 (4112S) and Special DeLuxe (4115S, 4120S).

16E: **Chevrolet** Series AG Sedan Delivery. All Chevy models now had 'Knee Action' IFS (with exposed coil springs) and steering column gear shift.

16C Chevrolet

16A Cadillac

16D Chevrolet

16B Cadillac

16E Chevrolet

17A Chrysler

17C DeSoto

17D Dodge

17B Chrysler Imperial

17A: **Chrysler** Saratoga Model C-30K Sedan. Fluid Drive was standard, Vacamatic semi-automatic transmission optional. Complete range: Royal C-28S and Windsor C-28W with 121½-in wb and 6-cyl. engine, Saratoga C-30K and New Yorker C-30N with 127½-in wb and 8-in-line.

17B: **Chrysler** Crown Imperial C-33 Sedan Limousine sold at $2795 and had power-operated windows, 145½-in wb and 140-bhp 323·5 CID 'straight-eight' engine.

17C: **DeSoto** DeLuxe S-8 Sedan. Running boards were optional extra. DeLuxe and Custom had 121½-in wb. Plymouth-based SP-12 had 117½-in wb and smaller engine (export).

17D: **Dodge** Luxury Liner Custom D-19C (shown) and DeLuxe D-19S had 119½-in wb, 91-bhp L-head Six engine. Also available was 117½-in wb D20 with 87-bhp power unit.

1941

18A: **Ford** also had new body styling and like Chevrolet this was retained, with minor detail changes, until 1948. There were five basic models: 11A Super DeLuxe, 11A DeLuxe, 11A Special, 1GA DeLuxe and 1GA Special. All had 114-in wb. 1GA models had L-head six-cyl. 90 HP engine; the others had the 90 HP V8. There were 15 body styles. Shown: Model 11A Super DeLuxe Coupé.

18B: Canadian militarized **Ford** 11A Fordor Sedan had special bumpers, radiator guard, roof rack and other mods.

18C: Canadian **Ford** C11AS 'Heavy Utility' staff car was militarized Model 11A-79A Station Wagon. Also produced in Canada was a modified version, designated C11ADF, which had a full-floating truck rear axle with exposed propeller shaft, semi-elliptic rear springs, and 9·00—13 tyres (see 18D and 19A).

18D: FM Alexander's soft-top conversion of Canadian **Ford** C11ADF Station Wagon, photographed at the British Ford Dagenham plant.

18A Ford

18C Ford (Canada)

18B Ford (Canada)

18D Ford (Canada)

19A: Another 'topless' conversion of Canadian **Ford** C1TADF, serving in North Africa. After conversion, only the driver's door could be opened.

19B: During 1941 **Ford** USA produced its own $\frac{1}{4}$-ton 4 × 4 design, designated Model GP (shown). From 1942 the Willys MB design was manufactured in large numbers as Model GPW ('W' for Willys). Picture shows Edsel B. Ford (on back seat) and General Charles H. Bonesteel during a cross-country demonstration with the first production GP.

19C: **Graham** Hollywood Sedan. One of the last Grahams produced. Bodywork was similar to that of the Hupmobile Skylark (see page 10).

19D: **Hudson** Super Six Sedan had 121-in wb, 102-bhp L-head six-cyl. engine. Eight-cyl. engine was also available. Body styling was not very different from 1940 model. A smaller model, the Hudson Six, had 116-in wb and a 92-bhp engine, but looked similar.

19A Ford (Canada)

19C Graham

19B Ford

19D Hudson

20A: Lincoln 16H had V12 engine and 125-in wb. The Fordor Sedan shown weighed 3936 lb approx. and measured 210 × 73½ in.

20B: Mercury 19A had 95-bhp V8 engine. Body styling closely followed that of the Ford but wheelbase was four inches longer, at 118 in. There were seven body styles, including a station wagon. Shown: Model 19A-73 Town Sedan.

20C: Nash 600 was a new car, featuring unitary body-cum-chassis construction. It replaced the earlier LaFayette series at the lower end of the Nash range. Shown is Model 4140 Sedan, one of eight body styles. Wheelbase was 112 in, price $870.

20D: Nash Ambassador Sedan was available as Six (Model 4160, shown) or Eight (4180). Several other body styles were also marketed. General appearance was not unlike 600, major exceptions being bumpers and rear fender (wing) cut-outs.

20A Lincoln

20C Nash

20B Mercury

20D Nash

21A: **Oldsmobile** in 1941 produced 230,703 cars (its highest figure so far), of which no fewer than 113,690 had Hydramatic drive. This year also saw the completion of the 2-millionth Olds. There were five series: 66, 68, 76, 78 and 98 (second figure indicated number of cylinders). Shown is a Series 98 Custom Cruiser Sedan.

21B: **Packard** 110 was restyled and now featured built-in headlights. There were Special and DeLuxe versions. In April the Packard Clipper was launched, with 'fadeaway' front fenders. In September this new styling was extended throughout the range, with conventional styling optional on Senior cars.

21C: **Packard** 120 4-door Touring Sedan sold at $1291. In 1941 Packard produced 66,906 cars and considerable quantities of marine engines (for US Navy PT boats) and RR Merlin aero engines. Car shown has survived in England.

21D: **Plymouth** featured battery in engine compartment, oil bath air cleaner, floating-type oil pump intake, door checks, and counterbalanced trunk lid. Two series: P-11 DeLuxe and P-12 Special DeLuxe (shown). Two-tone paint finish was becoming fashionable.

21A Oldsmobile

21C Packard

21B Packard

21D Plymouth

22A: **Pontiac** Custom Torpedo Eight, Series 1941-29, Four-Door Four-Window Sedan had 248·9 CID engine and 122-in wb. Bodywork was by Fisher and also used for some other GM cars. There were also DeLuxe (119-in) and Streamliner (122-in) models. All were available with 6- or 8-cyl. engine. Production this year totalled 330,061, making Pontiac the fifth largest car producer in the nation.

22B: **Pontiac** Streamliner Torpedo Eight Sedan Coupé.

22C: **Studebaker** President Custom Cruiser had 117-bhp 4-litre 8-cylinder in-line L-head engine. Production was up 12% over 1940 and highest (at 133,855) since 1928.

22D: **Studebaker** Champion Coupé.

22E: **Willys** Model 441 104-in wb Americar was new for 1941 and produced alongside the Model MA 'Jeep', with which it shared the famous Go-Devil engine.

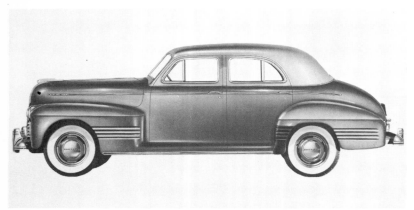

22A Pontiac

22C Studebaker

22B Pontiac

22D Studebaker

22E Willys

Although 1942 models had been introduced, as usual, in the late summer and autumn of the previous year, all production of civilian cars came to a halt on 9 February 1942. Production of civilian trucks halted on 3 March, the day after civilian car rationing commenced. Gasoline (petrol) rationing and a national speed limit followed, in order to conserve fuel and rubber. On the last day of 1941 the Automotive Council for War Production had been set up with the aim of applying the facilities of the automotive industry to all-out war production. Chrysler stepped up its production of tanks, spending $40 million on plant expansion, Ford opened the Willow Run Michigan Bomber Plant in May, General Motors produced countless items of war material including Chevrolet and GMC trucks, Nash-Kelvinator produced aircraft engines, helicopters, etc. Pontiac was the first automobile manufacturer to win the Navy 'E' Award, Chrysler's Tank Arsenal the first to win the Army-Navy 'E', which superseded it. Total value of arms produced by the automotive industry in 1942 was $4,665 million.

23B Buick

23A Buick

23C Buick

23A: **Buick** range had entirely new body styling. One-piece hood (bonnet) could be opened at either side and was quickly removable altogether.
23B: War-time **Buick** advertisement, showing 1942 Roadmaster Series 70 Convertible (Model 76-C). Super Model 56-C was similar in appearance but had 124-in vs 129-in wb.

23C: **Buick** Special Series 40 was cheapest range, on 118-in wb. Shown is the Model 48 Sedanet. Originally Buick offered 23 individual models for 1942, in six lines (Special, Extra Special (121-in wb), Super, Century, Roadmaster and Limited). Later this was reduced to 14 models. This 'H1942' range included seven Specials, three Supers, two Century's and three Roadmasters.

1942

24A: **Cadillac** Fleetwood Series 75 136-in wb Touring Sedan could be supplied with Formal Division (glass partition). It was Cadillac's top-line.

24B: **Cadillac** Fleetwood Seventy-Five with special coachwork, in use by the British RAF in the Far East (1948).

24C: **Cadillac** Series 62 Convertible. Fenders shown appeared on all 1942 Cadillacs, except Series 75. Convertible had full-width rear-seat. Series 61, 62, 63, 67 and 60S had Fisher bodies with Fleetwood interior styling.

24D: **Chevrolet** came in three series: BG Master DeLuxe, BH Special DeLuxe and Fleetline. Shown is a BG four-door sedan as used by the USMC. Wheel hub covers and other bright metal trim (except bumpers) of all US cars were painted instead of chrome as from 1 January 1942, by Government order.

24E: **Chevrolet** BH Special DeLuxe Coupé. Compared with 1941 the radiator grille was new and the front fenders extended onto the doors.

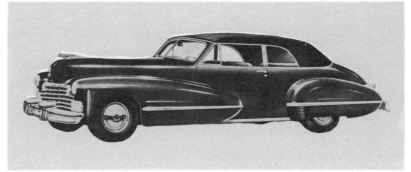

24C Cadillac

24D Chevrolet

24A Cadillac

24B Cadillac

24E Chevrolet

25A: **Chrysler** Royal C-34S and Windsor C-34W (shown, with Town & Country 6- or 9-seater bodywork) had 6-cyl. 250·6 CID engine and 121½-in wb. Fluid Drive and Vacamatic semi-auto. transmission were standard.

25B: **Chrysler** Saratoga C-36K and New Yorker C-36N (shown, with Convertible bodywork) had 8-cyl. 323·5 CID engine and 127½-in wb.

25C: **Chrysler** Crown Imperial C-37 had 145½-in wb and 8-in-line engine. Only 448 Imperials had been made when civilian car production stopped in February 1942.

25D: **DeSoto** DeLuxe S-10 and Custom S-10 (shown) constituted 1942 model range, available with various body styles, all on 121½-in wb and powered by 236·7 CID 115-bhp L-head engine.

25A Chrysler

25B Chrysler

25D DeSoto

25C Chrysler

1942

26A: **DeSoto** 1942 had 'Airfoil' headlights which in daytime were concealed behind sliding panels.

26B: **Dodge** marketed two lines, the DeLuxe D-22S and the Custom D-22C (shown). 68,522 of these 1942 models were produced until Dodge converted entirely to military truck production, chiefly the ¾-ton 4 × 4 'Beep'.

26C: **Dodge** DeLuxe D-22S '3-Window' Coupé. All models were available with Fluid Drive transmission.

26D: **Dodge** 1942 Sedan used by the military as a staff car. Note painted 'brightwork' instead of chrome (except bumpers) and blackout masks on headlights.

26A DeSoto

26C Dodge

26B Dodge

26D Dodge

27A: Ford 21A-73B Super DeLuxe Fordor Sedan. There were four series: 21A Super DeLuxe (V8), 21A DeLuxe (V8), 2GA DeLuxe (Six), and 2GA Special (Six). Both engines developed 90 bhp and all had 114-in wb. Body styles numbered 14.

27B: Ford 21A DeLuxe Fordor Sedan, used by British Forces in North Africa. Military modifications included 9·00—13 desert tyres, equipment racks and brackets, and a canvas-covered observation hatch in the roof.

British Army nomenclature: 'Cars, 4/5-Seater, Ford'.

27C: Hudson Super Six, Model 21. 1942 Hudsons differed from 1941 models only in minor details. Only 5396 Hudson cars and 67 commercials were delivered in 1942.

27D: Hudson stopped production of civilian cars on 5 February. Shown is the last one 'for the duration'. Most of the brightwork had austere paint finish.

27A Ford

27C Hudson

27B Ford

27D Hudson

1942

28A: **Lincoln-Zephyr** 26H had V12 L-head engine, restyled front end, and was optionally available with Liquamatic Drive automatic gearshift.

28B: **Lincoln** Continental 26H Cabriolet, Model 56, was one of Ford's top-line models. Its shipping weight was 4020 lb, price $3169. Coupé, Model 57, weighed 20 lb less but sold at same price.

28C: **Mercury** 29A had 118-in wb and was available as Sedan (29A-70), Sedan Coupé (72), Town Sedan (73), Club Convertible (76), 5-Window Coupé (77) and Station Wagon (79, shown).

28D: **Mercury** 29A-76 with desert tyres, used by 9th Australian Division in Middle East. Photo was taken at Gaza aerodrome, Palestine, in 1942.

28B Lincoln

Streamlining That Starts Away Down Deep

THERE's a definite feeling of depth and power in the flowing lines of the 1942 Lincoln-Zephyr, because its beauty is more than surface deep. ★ This modernness starts at the very core of the car! Built on an entirely new principle that sets it apart from other automobiles, the Lincoln-Zephyr is *naturally* streamlined right from its basic construction on through to its longer, lower appearance. ★ Free from excess weight . . . and with its V-type 12-cylinder engine more powerful than ever . . . this fine car gives you a different kind of ride. Relaxed on chair-high seats cradled amidships on longer, slow-motion springs, you skim along the highways with glider-like ease. ★ Interiors are roomy, more richly appointed this year. And the new Lincoln Liquamatic Drive with automatic gearshift* enables you to drive all day without shifting or even touching the clutch. ★ This is a good year to buy a better car. And the new Lincoln-Zephyr is truly the finest ever to bear the name. There's been no skimping on materials, no compromise with Lincoln traditions. The *quality* of the 1942 Lincoln-Zephyr also *starts away down deep!*

LINCOLN MOTOR CAR DIVISION, FORD MOTOR COMPANY
Builders of the Lincoln-Zephyr V-12, Sedan, Coupé, Club Coupe, Convertible Coupe; the Lincoln-Continental, Cabriolet and Coupe; the Lincoln-Custom, Sedan and Limousine.

*Optional at moderate cost

The Finest Lincolns Ever Built

Lincoln Zephyr V-12

28A Lincoln

28C Mercury

28D Mercury

29A: Nash 600, Model 4240 Sedan was one of five body styles available. Wheelbase was 112 in, engine 6-cyl. L-head. This sedan sold at $993.

29B: Nash Ambassador, last 'pre-war' model to come off the assembly line. The date: 4 February 1942.

29C: Oldsmobile had five series for the 1942 model year: 6-cyl. 66 and 76, 8-cyl. 68, 78 and 98. Prices ranged from $984 to $1307. Shown is a Hydramatic-equipped 98 Dynamic Cruiser Sedan.

29D: Packard Clipper 180 was first introduced in 1941 and carried-over for 1942 model year. 1946 Clipper (q.v.) was to be similar in appearance to 1941/42 model, main exception being the radiator grille.

29A Nash

29C Oldsmobile

29B Nash

29D Packard

1942

30A: **Packard** Clipper was available as Six or Eight (price difference $55) and either as Special or Custom model. Electromatic Drive (overdrive) optional.
30B: **Packard** Sedans were used by US Army as 'Automobile, Medium Sedan, 5-Passenger, 4 × 2'.
30C: This **Packard** Series 160 Limousine has survived in Great Britain. The last civilian 1942 Packard car was produced on 9 February.

One of two distinguished new versions of Clipper styling for 1942 — the smart Packard Clipper Touring Sedan. Both Clipper Six and Eight *(only $55 difference)* are available as either Special or Custom models.

How Clipper beauty pays off... in more miles per gallon!

1942 PACKARD CLIPPER

30A Packard

30B Packard

30C Packard

31A: **Plymouth** offered two lines: DeLuxe P-14S and Special DeLuxe P-14C. Both had 117½-in wb and 95-bhp 217 CID L-head power unit. They were in production from August 1941 to January 1942.

31B: **Plymouth** Special DeLuxe P-14C Convertible Coupé. New grille and integrated front fenders (wings) were notable styling changes from 1941 models.

31C: **Plymouth** period advertisement stressed economy and its being Chrysler Corporation's No. 1 car.

31A Plymouth

31B Plymouth

31C Plymouth

1942

32A: **Pontiac** offered 20 1942 models in four series: Torpedo Six 25, Streamliner Six 26, Torpedo Eight 27 and Streamliner Eight 28. Shown is a Torpedo Two-Door, available as Six or Eight (both with 119-in wb).
32B: **Pontiac** Torpedo Eight Series 27 four-door Sedan. Eights had 248·9 CID, Sixes 239·2 CID; both were L-heads.
32C: **Pontiac** Streamliner Series 26 (Six) (shown) or 28 (Eight)

Station Wagon. Wheelbase of all Streamliner models was 122 in. Other body styles in Streamliner Series were sedan coupé and four-door six-window sedan. Wagon shown was used by USMC.
32D: Last **Pontiac** to come off the line, early in 1942. Pontiac assembly plants were located in Atlanta, Linden, Oakland, Pontiac (main plant), St Louis, Southgate and Tarrytown.

32A Pontiac

32C Pontiac

32B Pontiac

32D Pontiac

33A: **Studebaker** offered three ranges of cars, the economical Champion, the Commander and the luxurious President 8. The latter two were offered with Turbomatic Drive (fluid coupling with controlled gear selection and automatic overdrive) as optional extra but few seem to have been delivered with this transmission.

33B: **Studebaker** Champion Custom Cruiser Sedan sold at $862 (DeLuxe version $897). This specimen was photographed in Spain some 20 years later.

33C: **Studebaker** body styling was known as Skyway. Shown is the attractive and fashionable four-door four-window Land Cruiser bodywork on the Commander chassis.

33A Studebaker

33B Studebaker

33C Studebaker

1943–45

All US civilian car and truck production came to a halt early in 1942. From then on all plants were fully engaged on war production, the volume of which had gradually increased from 1940. Not all automobile manufacturers produced military vehicles; many plants turned out aircraft engines and components, artillery shells, machine guns, AA guns and other munitions. In 1943 the Automotive Council for War Production announced that the automotive industry had supplied war material to the value of $13 billion and that 1038 automotive plants throughout the nation voluntarily co-operated to maintain maximum production. The Detroit region was shown accountable, in 1944, for 13·6 per cent of the nation's munitions output. In 1944 $9 billion worth of war material was produced and the cost to the Government had been reduced by one-third since 1941. In November 1944 the War Production Board authorized production of limited numbers of civilian trucks for essential non-military use. By the summer of 1945 many manufacturers commenced civilian car production again. What emerged were face-lifted 1942 models. At first only a few different body styles were released but the model availability was gradually extended to almost 1942 level. They were launched as 1946 models (q.v.).

34C Dodge

34A Chevrolet (Canada)

34B Crosley

34D Ford

34A: **Chevrolet** C8A-HUP (Heavy Utility, Personnel) was produced by General Motors of Canada to supersede the earlier Ford-built station wagons. The C8A was used as a personnel carrier, staff car, wireless truck, etc., with detail modifications to the standard box-shape body. Some 13,000 were produced, at about $1850 each. They had four-wheel drive (4 × 4) and were members of the family of Canadian Military Pattern (CMP) vehicles.

34B: **Crosley** CT-3 'Pup', one of several experimental light-weight military field cars produced in 1943. This survivor was discovered by the editor in Stamford, Conn., in 1967.

34C: **Dodge** T214 Command Car was built on the famous 'Beep' Weapons Carrier chassis. In back seat: King George VI, Lt.-General M. W. Clark (USA) and General Sir Harold R. L. G. Alexander.

34D: **Ford** GPA was amphibious version of GPW 'Jeep'. A small fleet of them are seen here churning their way down the Detroit River.

35A: **Willys** and **Ford** produced 361,349 and 277,896 units respectively of the standardized 'Jeep', which one war correspondent described as 'a divine instrument of wartime locomotion'. 'Jeep' later became a trademark for the Willys design and its successors and descendants.
35B: The 'Jeep' in action, 1943. (See also 'THE JEEP' in this series.)
35C: 'Jeeps' for the Canadian Army being camouflage-painted after assembly in England, 1942.
35D: Lt.-General Mark W. Clark riding past St Peter's in his 'Jeep' after the Allied capture of Rome, 4 June 1944. Major Generals Alfred M. Gruenther and Geoffrey Keyes accompanied him.

35A 'Jeep'

35B 'Jeep'

35C 'Jeep'

35D 'Jeep'

By the end of the war roughly ten million Americans were in the market for new cars. Most manufacturers had launched their 1946 models in the summer and autumn of 1945, but production was hampered by shortage of materials and by strikes. Nevertheless, the one-millionth post-war car was built in August, 1946, and there were several new cars, including the Kaiser and the Frazer which were produced in the Willow Run plant (used by Ford for bomber production during the war). Other new makes announced included Bobbi-Kar, Brogan, Comet, Darrin, Davis, Motorette, Playboy, Publix, Rocket, Super-Kar and Tucker. Their production, however, was minimal. The Automotive Golden Jubilee was celebrated in a big way in Detroit from 29 May to 9 June. Total production during 1945 and 1946 amounted to: cars, 1945: 69,532, 1946: 2,148,699, trucks and buses, 1945: 655,683, 1946: 940,866. Their combined total value was more than $4½ billion.

Yes, its Engine is still out Front

36B Buick

36A Buick

36A: **Buick** started its 1946 season in late 1945 with four Series 50 Super models (including an Estate Wagon, Model 59) and three Series 70 Roadmaster models. By mid-1946 two Series 40 Specials had reappeared. The Century Series 60 was dropped. Shown: Series 50 Super, Model 51 Sedan.
36B: **Buick** period advertisement.
36C: **Cadillac** offered four series: 61, 62, 60 Special and 75. Shown is the Series 62 Convertible Club Coupé. Engines were 150-bhp 346 CID V8s.

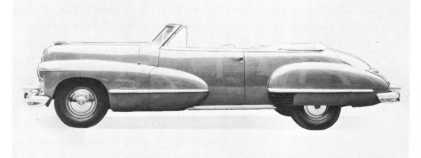

36C Cadillac

37A: **Cadillac** Fleetwood Series 75 7-passenger Touring Sedan was optionally available with dividing partition, for formal use. Wheelbase was 136 in. Hydramatic optional on all models.

37B: **Chevrolet** Stylemaster Series DJ Model 1503 Sedan. Except for grille, bumpers and emblems it was same as 1942. Also available were Series DK Fleetmaster and Fleetline models. Australian production comprised Victory Stylemaster 1200 and Victory Fleetmaster 1000 models.

37C: **Chevrolet** Fleetline Series DK Model 2144 Aerosedan.

37D: **Chrysler** Town & Country Convertible. The 1946 Chrysler range, which remained in production until February 1949, comprised the Royal C-38S and Windsor C-38W (6-cyl., 121½-in wb) and Saratoga C-39K and New Yorker C-39N (8-cyl., 127½-in wb). The Town & Country was available in five body styles on both the C-38W and the C-39N chassis and featured white ash with mahogany panels. C-40 Crown Imperial had 145½-in wb.

37A Cadillac

37C Chevrolet

37B Chevrolet

37D Chrysler

THERE'S A *Crosley* FOR YOU!

CROSLEY STATION WAGON

Seats four with plenty of luggage space. Rear seat removable. Entire rear end opens for easy loading. All steel—no wood to rot, swell, shrink or rattle.

CROSLEY CONVERTIBLE

Smartest thing on wheels! Carries four husky passengers plus baggage. Easy to manage laminated top snaps into place in a jiffy.

CROSLEY SEDAN

Needs no introduction. Thousands already on the road. Constantly improved in both beauty and performance. Styled with an "aircraft flavor." Four passenger. For all around use.

CROSLEY PICK-UP

Full quarter ton capacity. Drop tail gate. Roomy, comfortable cab. Amazingly economical. Cuts operating and delivery costs. Perfect for all service men, farms, city and country places.

CROSLEY PANEL DELIVERY

Want to save money on light deliveries? Grocers, druggists, dry cleaners—appliance, hardware and other service stores report sensationally low operating costs. Plenty of space for your advertisement on the sides.

CROSLEY SPORTS-UTILITY

A truly amazing value! Newest, and lowest priced of all Crosleys. Rear seat is available. Quarter-ton capacity for utility use. Fabric top and sides go on snug and tight in "no time."

SPECIFICATIONS

Overall Length	145 inches
Overall Width	49 inches
Overall Weight (with spare tire, gas, oil and water)	1155 pounds
Height	59 inches
Wheelbase	80 inches
Cruising Speed	50 m.p.h.
Gas Tank Capacity	6.5 gals.
Brakes	4 wheel
Type Brakes	Self-equalizing
Oil Capacity	2 quarts
Oil Filter Capacity	4/5 quart
*Body	All steel
Turning Radius	15 feet
Engine	Crosley COBRA
Cylinders	4
Cooling	Liquid
Type Engine	Valve-in-head
Horsepower	Up to 26.5
Compression Ratio	7½ to 1
Gasoline Mileage	35-50 m.p.g.
Tire Size	4.50 x 12 inches
Main Bearings	5
Lubrication	Pressure
Radiator	Tubular
Radiator Capacity	4 quarts
With Standard Heater	5 quarts

*Convertible and Sports-Utility have fabric tops.

CROSLEY
a FINE car

MANUFACTURED BY CROSLEY MOTORS, INC.
CINCINNATI 14, OHIO, U. S. A.

38A : Crosley, alias Crosmobile, had copper-brazed (COBRA) steel engine block.

39A: **Davis** was a new Californian three-wheeled 'fancy car' and seated four abreast. Few were made.

39B: **DeSoto** 9-passenger 139½-in wb Suburban featured folding third seat, roof luggage rack and duo-tone paint finish. Regular DeSoto models were the S-11 DeLuxe and Custom, both with 121½-in wb and 236·7 CID engines. There was also a special export model, based on the Plymouth and designated SP-15C Diplomat. 1946 model DeSotos were in production from November 1945 to February 1949.

39C: **Dodge** offered DeLuxe D-24S and Custom D-24C models on 119½-in wb, as well as a Plymouth-based export model with smaller engine, the D-25C Kingsway. The latter, with 117½-in wb, had the 217·8 CID 95-bhp engine (as Plymouth) as opposed to the 230·2 CID 102-bhp power unit of the regular models.

39B DeSoto

39A Davis

39C Dodge

1946

Smoother than ever – it's a new ride !

This new Ford car—so big and smartly styled—offers more new developments than most pre-war yearly models . . . New multi-leaf springs give you a ride that's smooth and level . . . Brakes, too, offer major new advancements. They're oversize, self-centering hydraulics for quick, quiet stops . . . There's stepped-up power—and new thrift in gas and oil . . . Inside, new luxury awaits you. Colorful fabrics and trim in pleasing two-tone combinations . . . Choose from two great engines. The V-8, now increased from 90 to 100 horsepower; the 90 horsepower Six . . . Ask your Dealer about the smartest Ford cars ever built.

FORD MOTOR COMPANY

TUNE IN . . . THE FORD SHOW . . . CBS, Tuesdays, 10-10:30 P. M., E.S.T. THE FORD SUNDAY EVENING HOUR . . . ABC, Sundays, 8-9 P. M., E.S.T.

THERE'S A *Ford* IN YOUR FUTURE

40A Ford

40A: **Ford** started 1946 model production on 6 July 1945. Advertising was directed at the (near) future.

40B: **Ford** offered two basic series, both in either DeLuxe or Super DeLuxe versions: 69A with 100-bhp V8 engine, 6GA with 90-bhp Six. Body styles numbered eleven. Shown is Model 73B Super DeLuxe Fordor Sedan. Cheapest model was 6-cyl. 3-passenger Coupé (71) at $947.

40C: **Ford** 69A-79B Super DeLuxe Station Wagon, surviving in Great Britain. Popularly known as 'Woodie'.

40B Ford

40C Ford

41A: **Hudson** Commodore Eight Sedan. Also available with six cylinder engine. Except for radiator grille they had same appearance as 1942 models. Their production started on 30 August 1945, and all had a 121-in wb chassis. The hood (bonnet) opened forward.

41B: **Kaiser** was first presented, in 1946, as a front-wheel drive car with unitary body/chassis and IFS/IRS (key: 1—engine; 2—clutch; 3—transmission; 4—final drive; A—stub axle; B—trailing arm; C—torsion bar, anchored at D). Production models, however, were of conventional design except for slab-sided bodywork (see 1947).

41C: **Lincoln** 66H was available as Sedan, Club Coupé and Convertible Coupé (shown in foreground). Also shown is the Lincoln Continental Coupé, which was priced at $4125. The Continental was also available with soft top.

41D: **Mercury** Eight 69M was available as Town Sedan, Sedan Coupé, Club Convertible (shown) and Station Wagon. Convertible was also available with wooden body panels (Sportsman). Post-war production of Ford's Mercury and Lincoln cars commenced on 1 November 1945.

41A Hudson

41C Lincoln

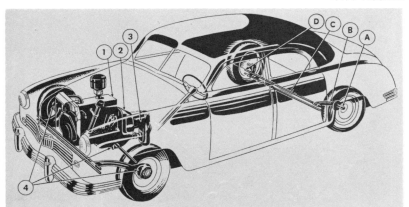

41B Kaiser

41D Mercury

1946

42A: **Nash** 600 had integral body/chassis unit and provided good fuel economy (up to 30 mpg). Nash sales in 1946 totalled 98,769 units, highest since the late 1920s. Model 4640 Sedan shown.

42B: **Nash** Ambassador Brougham Model 4663 looked like its counterpart in the 600 Series (Model 4643) but had 121-in (vs. 112-in) wheelbase and was easily distinguishable by its larger rear fender cut-outs. An 8-cyl. was not offered (as in 1942). In fact the first post-war

8-cyl. Nash was not introduced until 1955.

42C: **Nash** Ambassador, Model 4664. Several manufacturers, including Chrysler and Ford, offered cars with wooden body panels. This Nash was known as the Suburban and sold at $1929.

42D: **Oldsmobile** Series 98 Club Sedan had 8-in-line engine. Olds in 1946 sold 112,680 cars, including 12,891 Valiants for handicapped service men.

42A Nash

42C Nash

42B Nash

42D Oldsmobile

43A: **Packard** DeLuxe Clipper Sedan. First post-war Packard was built on 19 October 1945. 2721 followed. In 1946, 42,102 cars were produced. Material shortages, strikes in supplier plants and one strike at Packard resulted in loss of 75 working days. By June, 14 body types, eight chassis and three engines were offered.

43B: **Plymouth** DeLuxe P-15S and Special DeLuxe P-15C (shown) were produced from 1945 to 1949 with very little change. In export markets they were also sold as DeSoto Diplomat and Dodge Kingsway (with different grilles and badges).

43C: **Pontiac** Torpedo Eight, Series 27, Sedan had 248·9 CID engine, 119-in. wb. Also available as Six (Series 25). Six body styles.

43D: **Pontiac** Streamliner Eight, Series 28, Sedan Coupé had same engine as Torpedo, but 122-in. wb. Six was also available (Series 26). Three body styles.

The No. 1 Glamour Car of America

43A Packard

43C Pontiac

43B Plymouth

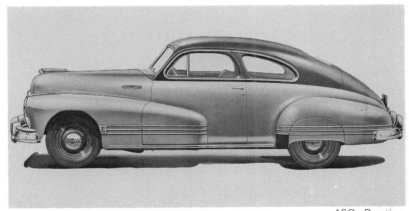

43D Pontiac

1946

44A Studebaker

44B Willys

44C Willys

44A: **Studebaker** first produced 'face-lifted' 1942 models, then in May, introduced the first real post-war Studebakers (see 1947), pioneering a new trend in car styling. The early 1946 models (shown) were all Skyway Champions. (3- and 5-passenger coupés, Club sedan and Cruiser sedan).

44B: **Willys-Overland** commenced production of the civilian 'Universal Jeep' in June 1945. During the rest of that year 1824 were made, followed by 71,455 in 1946. The 'Universal' Model CJ2A had sealed-beam headlights, steering column gearshift and a tailgate.

44C: **Willys-Overland** introduced its Model 4-63 4 x 2 Station Wagon in July 1946. It had seven seats (six from late 1947) and was kept in production virtually unchanged for several years.

In 1947 the automotive industry was in full swing again and sold almost as many vehicles as in 1941, namely 3,558,178 cars and 1,239,443 trucks and buses. The latter figure was the highest ever, so far. 266,795 cars and 263,351 trucks were exported. Kaiser-Frazer Corporation had bought the automotive assets of Graham-Paige and produced 11,753 cars in 1946, 144,506 in 1947, thus becoming the largest producer outside the Big Three. Preston Tucker produced a few pilot models of his revolutionary rear-engined car. Chevrolet opened new assembly plants in Flint, Michigan and Van Nuys, California, and introduced overhead assembly lines. Studebaker bought a wartime aircraft engine plant at South Bend. Two famous pioneers of the American automotive industry, William Crapo Durant (founder of General Motors) and Henry Ford both died in 1947. Canada banned import of US vehicles, but several makes were assembled or produced in Canadian subsidiaries of US companies.

In the US, driving education courses were adopted in many high schools.

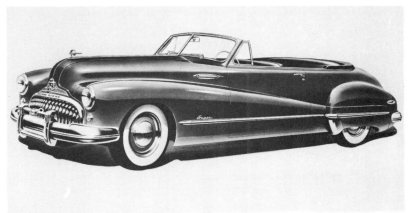

45B Buick

45A Buick

45C Buick

45A: **Buick** offered Special, Super and Roadmaster models, as in 1946. Except for the restyled radiator grille, they were substantially the same as the 1946 models. A Roadmaster Estate Wagon was added to the range, which now consisted of ten individual models. 1948 models were similar in appearance. Shown is a Series 40 Special Sedanet (RHD, produced in Canada), with 121-in. wb.

45B: **Buick** Series 50 Super Convertible, Model 56C, had hydraulically-operated top, door windows and front seat adjustment. Wb was 124 in.

45C: **Buick** Series 70 Roadmaster, Model 71, had 144-bhp 8-cyl. Fireball engine, 129-in. wb.

1947

46A: **Cadillac** Series 60S (Sixty Special) Sedan in Great Britain, where its taxable horsepower rating (RAC) was 39 HP.

46B: **Cadillac** Series 61 five-passenger Touring Sedan featured 'fastback' styling. Body by Fisher.

46C: **Cadillac** Series 62 was available as two- and four-door (shown) sedan and two-door convertible, selling at $2446, $2523 and $2902 respectively. Largest Cadillacs, priced up to $4887, were in Fleetwood 75 line.

46B Cadillac

46A Cadillac

46C Cadillac

47A: **Chevrolet** Series EJ Stylemaster two-door Town Sedan, Model EJ 1502. Other models in this series were coupés (3- and 5-passenger), a four-door sedan and a panel van (Model 1508 Sedan Delivery).
47B: **Chevrolet** Series EK Fleetmaster differed from EJ Stylemaster in that it was more luxurious. Shown is a Model EK2103 Sedan with RHD, surviving in Britain.
47C: **Chevrolet** Series EK Fleetline differed from Fleetmaster in body styling. This is the four-door Sportmaster Sedan, Model 2113. The other Fleetline model (Aerosedan, EK2144) was a two-door fastback coupé with lowered roofline and seat height. Both had distinctive triple mouldings on fenders.
47D: **Chrysler** and **Chrysler Imperial** models remained unchanged from preceding model year. Shown is the Crown Imperial C-40 Limousine on 145½-in. wb.

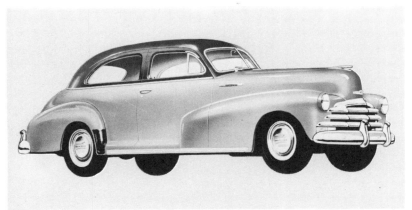

47A Chevrolet

47C Chevrolet

47B Chevrolet

47D Chrysler Imperial

1947

48A: **Chrysler** Imperial chassis with special coachwork by Derham.
48B: **DeSoto** Diplomat Special DeLuxe SP-15C was essentially a
Plymouth but had its own distinctive radiator grille. It was available for
DeSoto dealers overseas in order to have a low-priced car.

48C: **DeSoto** regular models (S-11) were the same as for 1946.
48D: **Dodge** D-24S DeLuxe and D-24C Custom were also the same as
for 1946. D-25C Kingsway had the same technical specification as
Plymouth and DeSoto Diplomat.

48A Chrysler Imperial/Derham

48C DeSoto

48B DeSoto

48D Dodge

49A: Ford 1947 models differed but slightly from 1946. Main exterior difference was reshaping and relocation of parking lights which were now circular and situated below the headlights. There were three basic series: 79A (100-bhp V8), 7GA (90-bhp Six) and 7HA (95-bhp Six). All had 114-in. wb and there were eleven body styles. Shown: Super DeLuxe Station Wagon (body type 79B).

49B: Frazer F47 Sedan was one of eight models offered by Kaiser-Frazer. This included a new luxurious model named Manhattan. Cars were of conventional design with Continental L-head Six engine but had advanced body styling (by Howard Darrin).

49C: Hudson Super Six Sedan. Also available were Super Eight, and Commodore Six and Eight, all on 121-in. wb. There were 12 models, priced from $1628 to $2196. Over 100,000 were produced.

49D: Hudson produced its three-millionth car in 1947. It is shown here alongside No. 1 of 1909.

49A Ford

49C Hudson

49B Frazer

49D Hudson

50A: Kaiser K100 Special Sedan was one of two models available and sold at $1868. Wheelbase was 123½ in., engine 226·2 CID Six. Other model was K101 Custom. Kaiser-Frazer Corp. employed some 21,000 people, mainly at their Willow Run plant near Ypsilanti, Michigan.
50B: Lincoln Continental 76H Cabriolet had 130-bhp 5-litre L-head V12 engine with hydraulic valve lifters. Price, at Detroit, was $4746.

50C: Mercury, like Lincoln, was substantially the same car as in 1946. Main exterior difference was shorter body side mouldings with separate name plates on hood (bonnet) sides. Series designation was 79M.
50D: Monarch was Canadian-built version of the Mercury and differed mainly in having its own distinctive grille. It was introduced in 1946 and continued virtually unchanged until 1948.

50A Kaiser

LINCOLN CONTINENTAL Cabriolet.

50B Lincoln

50C Mercury

50D Monarch

51A: **Nash** 600, Model 4740 Trunk Sedan had 'notchback' styling, unlike Model 4748 Slipstream Sedan which had 'fastback'. Third model available was 4643 Brougham.

51B: **Oldsmobile** Series 66 and 68 four-door sedans had 100-bhp 6-cyl. and 110-bhp 8-cyl. engines respectively but looked alike. Fisher body was also used for Chevrolet and Pontiac.

51C: **Packard** DeLuxe Eight Clipper was similar to 1946 equivalent and sold at $2124 (Club Sedan) and $2149 (Touring Sedan). They were designated 21st Series, Model 2111, had 120-in. wb and 282 CID L-head motor. Several other models, Sixes and Eights, were available.

51D: **Plymouth** Convertible was one of six body styles in Special DeLuxe range. DeLuxe range had four models. 1946 and 1948 models were similar.

51A Nash

51C Packard

51B Oldsmobile

51D Plymouth

52A: **Pontiac** Streamliner Sedan Coupé was available as Six (6MB) or Eight (8MB), both on 122-in. wb. In addition there were the Torpedo Six (6MA) and Eight (8MA) with 119-in. wb. 22 body styles were listed. Chassis were offered from $1046 (6MA).

General Motors of Canada produced their own Pontiacs, using Chevrolet bodyshells (e.g. Pontiac Fleetleader Special was basically Chevrolet Fleetline Aerosedan with distinguishing radiator grille, emblems, etc.)

52B: **Studebaker** Model 6G Champion Regal DeLuxe 5-passenger Coupé featured trend-setting 'coming-or-going' body styling by Raymond Loewy (introduced on Commander in May 1946). Wheelbase was 112 in., overall length 192¾ in., engine 170 CID Six.

52C: **Studebaker** Model 14A Commander Regal DeLuxe 6-passenger Sedan had 119-in. wb, 226·2 CID 6-cyl. engine. Top-line Land Cruiser model had same engine but 123-in. wb.

52A Pontiac

52B Studebaker

52C Studebaker

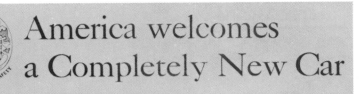

53A Tucker

53A: Tucker Corporation's Model 48 Sedan had rear-mounted 166-bhp horizontally-opposed six-cyl. engine, IFS, IRS, 128-in. wb, and was only five feet high. Centre 'Cyclops Eye' light turned with the front wheels. A few pilot models were built for public displays.

The following year it was announced that the first assembly line model was completed, but quantity production never came off the ground and in 1949 the firm was ordered by the Federal Court to return its leased Chicago plant to the War Assets Administration. The very few existing Tuckers are now prize possessions among car collectors.

53B: Willys continued production of the fast-selling 80-in. wb 'Universal Jeep', Model CJ2A, and the 4-63 'Jeep' station wagon which had 104-in. wb. Ex-works retail prices were $1146 and $1625 respectively. The auxiliary (7th) seat in the latter was discontinued late in 1947, with no change in price.

53B Willys

1948

During 1948 most manufacturers released their first real post-war models. Most of these were considered 1949 models (q.v.) but some were early enough to be shown here as 1948 models. Since no National Automobile Show had been staged since the Autumn of 1940, each manufacturer introduced its new models to the public as and when they were ready. Total factory sales figures were slightly up on 1947, with 3,909,270 cars and 1,376,274 trucks and buses. 217,911 cars were exported and many others were assembled in Canadian and overseas plants.

In August the nation's 100-millionth motor vehicle was completed. The 21-millionth Chevy and 5-millionth Buick were produced. General Motors' Australian affiliate (GM-H) introduced the Holden, Australia's first mass-produced car. It was an instant success. In addition, General Motors-Holden's continued assembling Canadian chassis (Chevrolet, Pontiac) fitting them with their own distinctive bodywork. Several well-known people in the US automotive industry died this year, including William S. Knudsen, Charles W. Nash and Nicholas Dreystadt. Great Britain, Canada and the US signed an agreement for standardization of threads, the ABC thread standard. Tubeless tyres were introduced by Goodrich.

54B Buick

54A Buick

54C Buick

54A: **Buick** Special, Series 40, came in two models: 41 Sedan (shown) and 46S Sedanet (fastback coupé; see 1947).
54B: **Buick** Super, Series 50, offered four body style options including this Model 51 Sedan. All 1948 Buicks were 'carryovers' from 1947.

Brand-new models were introduced in November.
54C: **Buick** Roadmaster Convertible, Model 76C, was one of four models in the Series 70. They were available, for the first time, with Dynaflow hyd. torque converter transmission.

55A: **Cadillac** introduced new models with distinctive rear fenders (wings). Shown is the Series 62 Sedan, Model 6269. It had a 346 CID V8 engine and 126-in. wb, like the less expensive Series 61. Series 60S had 133-in. wb.

55B: **Cadillac** Series 62 Convertible, Model 6267, sold at $3442. Convertible body style was not available in the other series (61, 60S, 75). Most expensive Caddy was Model 7533L Fleetwood 75 9-passenger, at $4863.

55C: **Checker Cab** of 1948/49 was sturdy, purpose-built car. Rear axle was set well back in relation to passenger compartment. It was also available as a conventional sedan ('pleasure car'). From 1921 until now Checker Motors had only produced taxicabs.

55D: **Chevrolet** had only minor modifications for 1948, including vertical centre moulding in radiator grille. Shown is Fleetline Series FK, Model 2113 Sportmaster Sedan. Stylemaster and Fleetmaster/Fleetline Series were designated FJ and FK respectively.

55A Cadillac

55B Cadillac

55C Checker Cab

55D Chevrolet

1948

56A: **Chrysler** 1948 models were similar to those of 1947 and 1946. Completely new models were introduced later in the year (see 1949).
56B: **DeSoto** models, too, were 'carryovers' from 1947. Shown is the S-11 Custom Sedan with 121½-in. wb.
56C: **Dodge**, like the other divisions of the Chrysler Corporation, continued production of existing models until early 1949, (although the

1949 models were first produced in December 1948). Both 117-in. and 119½-in. wb models were built.
56D: **Ford** 89A (100-bhp V8) and 8HA (95-bhp Six) were similar to 1947 79A and 7HA respectively, and available in either DeLuxe or Super DeLuxe form. Ten body types were listed. Ford's real post-war (1949) models were unveiled in June.

56A Chrysler

56C Dodge

56B DeSoto

56D Ford

57A: **Frazer** offered two models, the basic F485 and the Manhattan F486. Both were six-passenger four-door Sedans with 226·2 CID L-head Continental Six and 123½-in. wb. List prices were $2321 and $2573 respectively.

57B: **Hudson** was one of the first manufacturers to unveil post-war models, in December 1947. They featured a box-section chassis frame built into the body and extending outside the rear wheels. Called 'Monobilt', the floor was well below the door sills. Shown is the new Commodore Sedan being televised. Television was still in its infancy.

57C: **Kaiser**, like its companion make Frazer, offered two 123½-in. wb

four-door sedans, the basic K481 and the Custom K482. Mechanically all four were similar.

57D: **Keller** was a new firm, located at Huntsville, Alabama. They offered two models, the Super Chief Station Wagon (shown) and convertible. For the latter there was a choice of engine location, front or rear. This power unit was a 49-bhp 4-cyl. Continental. Suspension was independent, front and rear, with trailing arms and rubber spring units. Later a smaller Hercules 47-bhp engine was made available (Chief models).

57A Frazer

57C Kaiser

57B Hudson

57D Keller

58A: Lincoln 1948 models (876H) were in production from November 1947 to April 1948 and were similar to 1947 models. On 20 April a new range was launched. Of these, the 9EL Sport Sedan is illustrated. V12 engines were discontinued. (See also 1949.)

58B: Mercury also continued its 1947 models practically unchanged (but redesignated 89M) until new models were introduced on 29 April 1948 (see 1949). Shown is a 1947–48 Station Wagon, converted as ambulance. Engine was 239·4 CID V8, wheelbase 118 in.

58C: Monarch, Ford of Canada's Mercury-based car continued virtually unchanged until later in the year.

58D: Nash Ambassador Super Sedan. Nash in 1948 offered seven 600 models, eight Ambassadors (four Super, four Custom). Completely new models were displayed in September.

58A Lincoln

58C Monarch

58B Mercury

58D Nash

59A: **Oldsmobile** Series 70 Dynamic was available with either six-cyl. (Model 76) or eight-cyl. (Model 78) engine, both on 125-in. wb chassis. 119-in. wb Dynamic Series 60 models were also offered (66 Six and 68 Eight). Hydramatic drive was optional extra.
59B: **Oldsmobile** celebrated its 50th anniversary in 1948 and introduced its new Futuramic models in the Series 98. Convertible, two-door Club sedans and four-door sedans (shown) were available.
59C: **Packard** introduced an entirely new model in 1948. New York's school of styling and design, Fashion Academy, voted it its gold medal of honour for being 'new, modern, smart and yet elegantly simple'.

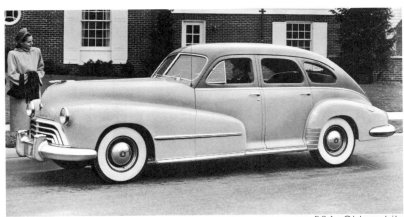

59A Oldsmobile

59B Oldsmobile

59C Packard

60A: **Playboy**, produced by the Playboy Motor Car Corp., was 'the Nation's Newest Car Sensation'. This company was formed by Lou Horwitz, Charles D. Thomas and Normand Richardson, in Buffalo, NY. The car had a metal convertible top and a Continental 4-cyl. engine. Automatic transmission was optional.

60B: **Plymouth** Special DeLuxe P-15C was a carryover from 1947. So was the DeLuxe P-15S. Their total production run was from October 1945 to February 1949.

60C: **Pontiac** offered four Silver Streak series in 1948: 6PA Torpedo Six, 6PB Streamliner Six, 8PA Torpedo Eight and 8PB Streamliner Eight. Torpedo models had 119-in., Streamliners 112-in. wb. There were 15 body styles. Illustrated is the DeLuxe Torpedo Eight Convertible.

60D: **Pontiac** DeLuxe Streamliner Eight Sedan. All 1948 Pontiacs could be ordered with Hydramatic drive, at extra cost.

60A Playboy

60C Pontiac

60B Plymouth

60D Pontiac

61A: **Studebaker** Champion 7G Regal DeLuxe Sedan. Compared with 1947 the new Champion had horizontal mouldings added to the outer radiator grilles and restyled bumpers. There were four DeLuxe and five Regal DeLuxe models, all with 112-in. wb.

61B: **Studebaker** Commander 15A Regal DeLuxe featured small changes in comparison with preceding 14A (added moulding above grille, revised bumpers). 15A Series comprised nine Commanders (four

DeLuxe, five Regal DeLuxe) with 119-in. wb and one Land Cruiser, with 123-in. wb.

61C: **Willys** extended its line of 'Jeep' vehicles and displayed here around the 'Universal Jeep' in front of the Toledo administration building are, from left to right, the 4-63 Station Wagon, CJ2A Fire Fighter, 2WD Platform/Stake Truck, 4-63 Panel Delivery, 4WD Pick-up, 6-63 Station Sedan and VJ3 Jeepster Phaeton.

61A Studebaker

61C Willys

61B Studebaker

1949

The 1949 models of all major manufacturers were the first true post-war models. Practically all of them had been introduced during 1948, a few even earlier, to supersede the 1946/47 models which had been, in fact, facelifted versions of the cars produced in 1941/42. Public acceptance of these new cars was reflected in their sales figures which, totalling 5,119,466, were more than 1·2 million higher than for 1948. Export of complete cars was down to just over 140,000 units, but assembly of US cars with incorporation of locally-made parts and materials took place in a number of overseas countries. US production of trucks and buses amounted to 1,134,185 units. The American Trucking Association reported that about 60% of the total freight transport in the US was now carried by trucks. The US automotive industry in its totality turned out over 6¼ million vehicles, thereby breaking its own 20-year old annual production record. Buick introduced a hard-top body style, soon to be followed by other auto makers. This type of pillar-less sedan, usually in two-door form, became very popular throughout the world.

62A Buick

62A: **Buick** Series 50 Super, Model 51 Sedan, 'popularity bellwether' of the Buick line. 'Portholes' were first used on 1949 models and remained a Buick feature for many years.
62B: **Buick** Series 70 Roadmaster, Model 76R Riviera (hardtop) Coupé made its appearance in June as an additional model. All Roadmasters had four 'portholes' (three on other series). A new Special line was introduced in August (Models 43, 46, 46S).
62C: **Cadillac** Series 62, Model 6269 Trunk Sedan. A Coupé DeVille model (hardtop) was added to the line in July. Other series: 60, 61, 75.

62C Cadillac

63A: Chevrolet introduced its first post-war models, in Series GJ Special (1500) and GK DeLuxe (2100). Of both there were Styleline ('bustleback') and Fleetline ('fastback') versions. All had 115-in. wb and the familiar six-cylinder OHV 216·5 CID engine. Shown is the Series GK DeLuxe Styleline Sedan, Model 2103.

63B: Chrysler models were completely new and came in two basic series: C-45 (Six) Royal and Windsor, and C-46 (Eight) Saratoga, New Yorker and Town & Country. Shown is a Royal nine-passenger Station Wagon. The body sheet metal was covered by a special photographic transfer process, simulating highly polished mahogany.

63C: Chrysler Crown Imperial C-47 had same wheelbase and engine as preceding C-40 but shared new body styling with other Chryslers. All Imperials had disc brakes.

63D: Crosley CD models featured many modifications and improvements ('hundreds', it was claimed.) They now had a cast-iron engine block (CIBA engine) and Hawley-designed Goodyear disc brakes. In addition to five CD models, there was the Model VC Hotshot two-seater Roadster, designed by Count Alexis de Sakhnoffsky and selling at $849. Most Crosley prices were under $900.

63A Chevrolet

63C Chrysler Imperial

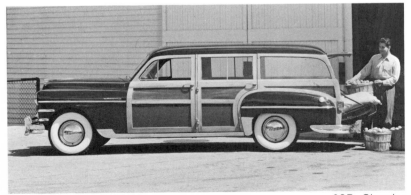

63B Chrysler

63D Crosley

1949

64A: **DeSoto** Custom (shown) and DeLuxe S-13 had new bodywork and 125½-in. wb. Their 236·7 CID L-head six-cylinder engine developed 112 bhp at 3600 rpm. Like other 1949 Chrysler Corp. cars they had key-operated ignition/starter switch. SP-18 Diplomat models had 118½-in. wb and different grille.

64B: **Dodge** offered four series on three wheelbases: the Wayfarer D-29 (115-in. wb), the Coronet and Meadowbrook D-30 (123½-in. wb), and the Kingsway D-32C (118½-in. wb). Shown is the Wayfarer Sportabout, a temporary revival of the roadster type, featuring take-out door

windows (later production had conventional crank-up windows).

64C: **Ford** announced its first real post-war models in June 1948. There were two series: 98HA (Six) and 98BA (V8), both on 114-in. wb. Standard and Custom versions were available in a variety of slab-sided body styles. For the first time Fords had IFS, with coil springs, replacing the old transverse leaf suspension. The rear axle was suspended on conventional leaf springs and the prop shaft exposed.

64D: **Ford** Custom two-door Sedan Model 70B was, as usual, designated Tudor (four-door was Fordor).

64A DeSoto

64C Ford

64B Dodge

64D Ford

65A: **Frazer** had dual-manifold engine, developing 112 bhp. Shown is the Model F496 Manhattan Sedan.

65B: **Hudson** Convertible. 1949 Hudsons were virtually similar to the previous year's models. There were four series: 491 Super Six, 492 Commodore Six, 493 Super Eight and 494 Commodore Eight.

65C: **Hudson** Commodore Six four-door Sedan had 124-in. wb, as had all other models. Six-cylinder engine was 262 CID L-head.

65D: **Kaiser** offered two series, the K491 Special and the K492 DeLuxe. Among the individual models were Traveller, Vagabond and Virginian sedans, and a convertible in the DeLuxe range. All were four-door six-seaters on 123½-in. wb with Continental 226·2 CID L-head Six engine.

65A Frazer

65C Hudson

65B Hudson

65D Kaiser

1949

66A: **Lincoln** produced two lines, the 9EL (Coupé, Sedan and Convertible, wb 121 in.) and the 9EM Cosmopolitan (Coupé, Sport Sedan, Town Sedan, and Convertible, wb 125 in.). V8 engines only were offered. Hydramatic was optional. Illustrated is the 9EM Cosmopolitan Sport Sedan. (For 9EL see 1948.)

66B: **Mercury** offered one range, designated 90M, and four body styles: Coupé (72), Sport Sedan (74, shown), Convertible (76) and Station Wagon (79). All had 118-in. wb and 255·4 CID V8 engine.

French Ford Vedette had similar body styling (except at rear).

66C: **Meteor** 58 was sold by Canadian Lincoln-Mercury dealers, replacing the earlier Mercury-based Monarch 114 (1946–48). It was introduced on 29 June 1948, in Coupé, Tudor and Fordor form, and was similar to the US Ford except for distinctive grille and trim features.

66D: **Monarch** name was continued by Ford of Canada for Canadian version of US Mercury. It was a higher-class car than the previous Monarch models (see also Meteor).

66C Meteor

66B Mercury

66A Lincoln

66D Monarch

67A: Nash 600 was available in nine versions (Special, Super and Custom two- and four-door sedans, and broughams) and had completely new bodywork, known as Airflyte. Engine was 172·6 CID Six, wheelbase 112 in. All nine models were also available as Ambassador, with 234·8 CID Six engine and 121-in. wb.
67B: Oldsmobile Series 76 DeLuxe Sedan, Model 3569D. All Olds 1949 models had the new Futuramic body styling. Series 76 had 257 CID L-head Six, 119½-in. wb.

67C: Oldsmobile Series 88 was basically similar to 76 but powered by 303·7 CID eight-cylinder engine. Oldsmobile's top-line was Series 98, with 125-in. wb.
67D: Packard 22nd Series was produced during 1948 and early 1949. The 23rd Series started on 2 May 1949. Illustrated is a DeLuxe Eight, Model 2211-9 Sedan, with 120-in. wb and 288 CID engine. Many others were available (ten ranges, 20 models). Custom models had additional vertical mouldings in grille and front bumper.

67A Nash

67C Oldsmobile

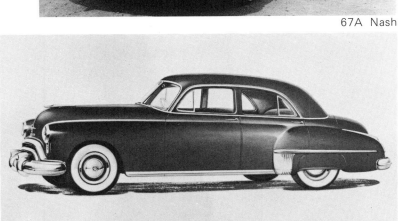

67B Oldsmobile

67D Packard

68A: **Plymouth** also offered its first real post-war models. There were two basic series, the P-17 DeLuxe with 111-in. wb and the P-18 DeLuxe and Special DeLuxe with 118½-in. wb. All had the familiar 217·8 CID L-head Six engine which now developed 97 bhp at 3600 rpm. Shown is a P-18 Special DeLuxe 8-passenger Station Wagon.

68B: **Plymouth** P-18 DeLuxe was available as 6-passenger Club Coupé and 6-passenger four-door Sedan (shown).
68C: **Plymouth** P-17 DeLuxe 5-passenger all-steel Station Wagon had one (folding) rear seat.

The car that likes to be compared—**new Plymouth**

If you prize value, Plymouth is the winner in the low-priced field. Of 22 quality features found in most high-priced cars, low-priced Plymouth has 21 — low-priced car "A" has 13 — low-priced car "B" has 4! See the new Quality Chart at your Plymouth dealer's now. Then — better still — drive all three of these cars. Let actual comparison on the road be your guide to the most dollar-for-dollar, feature-for-feature car value. PLYMOUTH Division of CHRYSLER CORPORATION, Detroit 31, Michigan

68A Plymouth

68B Plymouth

68C Plymouth

69A: **Pontiac** Silver Streak models shared Fisher bodywork with other GM products. Illustrated is a DeLuxe Sedan, Model 25-2569D.

69B: **Pontiac** Silver Streak Chieftain two-door Sedan. All 1949 Pontiacs had 120-in. wb. Engine was 239·2 CID Six for 6R Series, 248·9 CID Eight for 8R Series.

69C: **Pontiac** Silver Streak 8, Series 8R DeLuxe Streamliner Sedan Coupé.

69D: **Pontiac** Silver Streak 8, Series 8R Chieftain DeLuxe Sedan. Sun visor, radio and WSW tyres were among the optional extras.

69A Pontiac

69C Pontiac

69B Pontiac

69D Pontiac

1949

70A Studebaker

70A: **Studebaker** Champion Regal DeLuxe Sedan, Series 8G. 1949 Champions featured slight styling changes to radiator grille and bumper overriders, to distinguish them from the 1948 models. There were coupés (3- and 5-passenger), two- and four-door sedans, and a convertible.

70B: **Studebaker** Commander Regal DeLuxe Convertible, Series 16A. Commanders differed from 1948 editions in having restyled bumpers, addition of ornaments on top of front fenders, and more engine power. Automatic hill holder in transmission was standard (optional on Champion).

70C: **Willys** Model VJ2 and VJ3 Jeepsters were 'Jeep'-inspired phaetons on Model 4-63 104-in. wb 4-cyl. Station Wagon chassis. Engine was 134 CID L-head Four. Willys-Overland also produced a 6-cyl. (148 CID) Station Wagon, Model 6-63, and the Jeepster was available on this chassis as Model VJ3-6.

70C Willys

70B Studebaker

ABBREVIATIONS

bhp	brake horsepower
CID	cubic inch displacement (piston displacement in cubic inches)
cu in	cubic inch (= 16·39 cc)
IFS	independent front suspension
IRS	independent rear suspension
in	inch (= 2·54 cm)
L-head	side-valve (engine)
ohv	overhead valves
PAB	power-assisted brakes
q.v.	*quod vide* (which see)
RHD	right-hand drive
SAE	Society of Automotive Engineers
wb	wheelbase
WSW	white side walls (tyres)

SUMMARY OF MAJOR AMERICAN CAR MAKES

1940–49 (WITH DATES OF THEIR EXISTENCE)

CHRYSLER GROUP

Chrysler	(from 1923)
Chrysler Imperial	(from 1926)
DeSoto	(1928–60)
Dodge	(from 1914)
Plymouth	(from 1928)

FORD GROUP

Ford	(from 1903)
Lincoln	(from 1920)
Mercury	(from 1938)
Meteor (Canada)	(1948–61)
Monarch (Canada)	(1946–61)

GENERAL MOTORS GROUP

Buick	(from 1903)
Cadillac	(from 1903)
Chevrolet	(from 1911)
LaSalle	(1927–40)
Oldsmobile	(from 1896)
Pontiac	(from 1926)

NON-AFFILIATED MANUFACTURERS

American Bantam	(1930–41)
Checker	(from 1921)
Crosley	(1939–52)
Frazer	(1946–51)
Graham (-Paige)	(1927–41)
Hudson	(1909–57)
Hupmobile	(1908–41)
Kaiser	(1946–55)
Nash	(1917–57)
Packard	(1899–1958)
Studebaker	(1902–66)
Willys (-Overland)	(1908–63)

ACKNOWLEDGEMENTS

This book was compiled and written largely from historic source material in the library of the Olyslager Organisation, and in addition photographs and/or other material was kindly provided or loaned by the following organisations and individuals:

American Motors Corporation, Chrysler Corporation (USA and Canada), Ford Motor Company (USA, Canada and Great Britain), General Motors (USA, Canada and Great Britain), Imperial War Museum, etc., and several private collections, notably those of Jan Bakker, G. A. Ingram, Fred J. van Leeuwen, William F. Murray, Jan Polman, Stanley C. Poole, Bart H. Vanderveen and Laurie A. Wright.

INDEX